# THE NATI

G000096686

## THE PRO

# DORMANT POWERS OF THE GOVERNMENT:

## THE CONSTITUTION A CHARTER OF FREEDOM, AND NOT "A COVENANT WITH HELL:"

By EDWARD F. BULLARD,

AUTHOR OF THE LAW OF TRUSTS AND TRUSTEES.

---

**DEATH TO SLAVERY—LIFE TO THE REPUBLIC.**

---

NEW YORK:

C. B. RICHARDSON, HISTORICAL BOOKSELLER AND PUBLISHER,

594 and 596 Broadway.

ALBANY:

W. C. LITTLE, LAW PUBLISHER.

1863.

# THE NATION'S TRIAL:

## THE PROCLAMATION:

# DORMANT POWERS OF THE GOVERNMENT:

### THE CONSTITUTION A CHARTER OF FREEDOM, AND NOT "A COVENANT WITH HELL:"

By EDWARD F. BULLARD,

AUTHOR OF THE LAW OF TRUSTS AND TRUSTEES.

---

**DEATH TO SLAVERY—LIFE TO THE REPUBLIC.**

---

NEW YORK:

C. B. RICHARDSON, HISTORICAL BOOKSELLER AND PUBLISHER,
594 & 596 Broadway.

ALBANY:

W. C. LITTLE, LAW PUBLISHER.

1863.

TO THE CONSCIENTIOUS AND THINKING PUBLIC

THIS WORK

IS RESPECTFULLY DEDICATED

BY THE AUTHOR.

# PREFACE.

THE substance of the following Treatise was delivered as a lecture, first before the Young Men's Association of Waterford, February 18, 1863, and afterwards repeated at other places.

At the request of many members of the Bar, and others, it is published, after having been somewhat enlarged.

This work is published to awaken inquiry, as the present crisis seemed to demand a brief work upon the duties of the hour.

WATERFORD, N. Y., *April*, 1863.

# CONTENTS.

# CHAPTER I.

## FREEDOM AND MORAL IDEAS, THE MEASURE OF MAN'S PROGRESS.

WAR, with all its horrors, is trying this nation in the presence of the God of Justice.

When, in the course of events, a people apparently prosperous and happy, by domestic convulsions is deluging the country with blood, it becomes us to ascertain the *cause* and apply the *remedy.*

Progress is the law of the universe.

Science has demonstrated that animal life has existed on this planet for a thousand centuries, yet man has left recorded history reaching back less than six thousand years.

Although, in the beginning man was created after the image of God—that is, with a capacity to learn and exist forever—yet man remains but a poor representation of the God-head until his intellect has been cultivated and his affection born anew, so that he shall perceive *truth* and *love the right.*

In tracing the development of the human race, each individual must be treated as a trinity, that is: First, as a *physical;* second, as an intellectual ; third, as a moral being.

Until each of these attributes is developed, man is not truly seen in the image of his Creator.

Hence triumphs of art, which may call out and expand the physical and intellectual, do not necessarily develop the moral. In the former, Thebes and Nineveh excelled, yet they have perished and left nothing as an example to make us better, unless we take warning from their shortcomings.

If the end of man's existence was merely to build stately works of art, wear purple and fine linen, with no reference to an eternal destiny, then, indeed, was Egypt a great people before the book of Genesis was written, and our own America, two years since, had nearly become her equal.

But such was not the design of the great Father in creating man. He made him for a higher and nobler purpose,—to be educated, to exist and unfold forever.

Progress is an inherent law of the soul, and is written upon all created things. To avoid misunderstanding we use the term man as including all beings, without regard to color, that have souls within them, susceptible of improvement and capable of a future existence. Few, among the enlightened, can be found so ignorant or perverted by education as to deny 'to the African either of these qualities, or that he is capable of becoming " God's noblest work, an honest man."

The greatest benefactor to mankind, therefore, is he who serves God by improving the condition of his children.

Moral ideas are greater than works of art.

All ideas are promulgated to the world as mere words uttered or recorded.

The building of its cities has not done so much to advance the world as Paul's sermon on Mars Hill.

No one is so obscure as to be without his influence in raising or degrading the moral condition of his neighbor. Yet but few have become so high and pure as to leave their good works apparent to the whole world.

The mere *words* of those few have become the property of mankind, and they illuminate his pathway in the conflict between truth and error, right and wrong, as the sun illuminates the material universe.

But few persons, having the opportunity even, have so lived as to exhibit their characters so perfected and elevated as to become the light of the world.

But few events have become the great monuments which are known and read of all men.

The first of these was the life of Moses, who was born but 3,434 years since.

He astonished the world by the high moral standard which he raised, but did not live to see many of his own followers appreciate the scope of his teachings.

Where is the man who will now assert that his mere *words* or fanatacism have not been of more benefit to mankind than all the pyramids ever devised by the intellect or reared by the hand of man ?

The next of those events, which all civilized nations recognize, is the life and teachings of the humble Nazarene.

But little understood by the wisest of our day and generation, when on earth less than nineteen hundred years since, the wise men and rulers of that day heeded him not. Yet the mere IDEAS uttered by him have done more than all the armies, powers and inventions of the race to elevate mankind. In comparison with them, the conquests of Alexander and Cæsar are as grains of sand.

With all the light shed upon the world by him, but little, if any, progress was made by the masses for the first fifteen hundred years after they had crucified his body.

During that period, however, millions nominally professed his doctrines, and most of the nations of Europe claimed to rule in his name.

Eleven hundred years after the sermon on the mount, "the English were generally in the habit of selling their children and other relations to be slaves in Ireland, without having the pretext of distress or famine, till the Irish, in a national synod, agreed to emancipate all the English slaves in the Kingdom." (3 *Hallam, Middle Ages*, 371.)

In the year 1214, a few of the higher intellects of England wrung from King John, Magna Charta, whereon by degrees that nation has finally reared a high development of civilization.

Before they practically carried into effect, to any considerable extent, the principles announced by that great charter, that nation had to wade through turmoil and blood, for five centuries.

Long after its promulgation, tyranny and despotism continued hunting out victims for the stake and the rack, until the better portion of humanity looked in vain for an asylum upon the known globe.

In this dark hour, October 11, 1492, another great event startled mankind. On that day Columbus discovered the new world.

In his wisdom the Creator has seemingly reserved this continent to be the garden of his New Jerusalem and the school house of his people.

When the old world had become so corrupt and down-trodden, that practically, christianity had no place to lay its head, the Almighty inspired the great soul of Columbus to seek out this new continent as an asylum for the oppressed.

The spirit of tyranny after this time continued to run so high that the friends of man were crucified or banished to this continent.

Freedom of thought or religious toleration was not permitted in the old world.

Experience has shown that no people will become developed to a full manhood where freedom of speech is not tolerated.

Although Jesus had distinctly taught the equality of all men, and the divine right of the *indivdual* to freedom, yet up to that age his doctrine had been practically ignored. The state and church were everything—man was nothing.

It was after this and on the 10th of December, 1520, that Luther asserted a degree of religious freedom by burning the bull of the Pope.

But while the oppressions in the east were preparing the good seed to be sent to the new world, Satan was not idle.

Those who worshipped money and other material things, instead of God and his attributes of justice and truth, settled Jamestown, Virginia, in 1608, and soon after brought slavery with them. The friends of right were behind and did not land at Plymouth until December 22d, 1620.

The spirit of freedom began to gain power, so far as the white race was concerned, in England, and the result was the beheading of Charles I., in January, 1649.

Although the iron soul of Cromwell for a time nominally sustained the rights of the masses, yet the latter were not sufficiently educated to walk alone after their leader was taken from them.

The reaction in England again brought into power the conservatives, who soon hunted out of the kingdom many of her noblest souls.

The last hope of man now seemed centered upon the colonies of America.

After more than a hundred years of contest in this wilderness with the elements and in war, after going through more of hardship than did the children of Israel in Egypt, finally a portion of our people were aroused to assert some of their God-given rights.

The declaration of the equality of all men, July 4, 1776, was the outbirth of those times, and makes an era in the history of the world, which must be handed down to all future generations, while man shall deserve freedom and record history.

The great soul of Jefferson seemed inspired for the occasion, and he attempted, for the first time, to build a foundation for a nation upon the laws of God, which should deserve to be called a christian government.

# CHAPTER II.

## Our Defiance of God and his Justice.

LET us consider how far short we have come from practically carrying into effect these great principles.

Since this country established its separation from Great Britain, its strides in material greatness and intelligence have been the wonder of modern times.

General education has been diffused among the greater portion of the white race.

The power of invention has outrun the most vivid imagination.

The privileged class travel with ten times more speed and comfort than of old, and their messages are sent on the wings of lightning.

In our vast strides we have said: What next can come? what shall surprise us?

That next has come, and God has asked us if we have obeyed his laws, and been just to his children?

Jesus taught that God was represented in every man. Hence the saying:—" I was in prison and ye came unto me." "Inasmuch as ye have done it unto one of the least of these my brethren, ye have done it unto me."

Every man has the right to educate himself, and perfect his soul for a future and eternal existence.

Even Calhoun admitted this doctrine substantially, when he says:

" I assume as an incontestible fact, that man is so constituted as to be a social being. * * * In no other state could he attain to a full development of his moral and intellectual faculties, or raise himself in the scale of being much above the level of the brute creation."

Therefore any man, state, institution or nation which deprives the poorest, blackest or weakest man of those God-given rights, is directly fighting against God and his laws, and will sooner or later find it hard " to kick against the pricks."

" For whatsoever a man soweth, that shall he also reap."

Judged by this standard, are we practicing christianity ?

We speak of the whole nation, North and South. We must assume our share of guilt according to our light and opportunity.

Because, if those residing at the North have more light, so much more their responsibility.

If we have the ten talents and bury them, so much the lower must be our fall.

If we are blessed with knowledge and wisdom—see the evil and proclaim it not, but hide our light under a bushel—so much worse will be our condition, and seven devils will return in place of our one. Because, the greater the light, the greater the condemnation. Every one's experience has taught him this.

Thus, we should not blame the poor and ignorant in our midst, when but few of our educated lawyers, savans and clergy speak the truth boldly, and let their light shine before the world.

If any authority is needed, Paul, on Mars Hill, declared: " The times of this ignorance God winked at."

A practice that was comparatively a small evil in one condition of the world, under greater light and progress becomes a fatal one, which will overthrow a nation.

The same with nations as with individuals.

Tried by this standard, the leading men of this nation are educated at least equal to any that ever lived.

We have the benefit of the full light of christianity.

We have the example of that MAN who is the light of the world.

With such knowledge, we have no cloak for our wickedness. Hence the time has arrived when we, as a nation and a people, must choose between right and wrong—between God and the devil.

Paul, speaking to the learned men of Athens, says:

" Because he hath appointed a *day* in the which he will judge the world in *righteousness* by that man whom he hath ordained." (17 *Acts.*)

That day is upon this nation *now.*

That day was upon Babylon long ago.

She was judged and found wanting.

That day was upon Jerusalem when she heard Jesus, but refused to follow his precepts and practice truth and right.

What is Babylon now ? A desert.

What Jerusalem ? A den of thieves.

It is therefore apparent that no people can be truly christian until they live up to that standard which requires them to do unto others as they would have others do unto them.

We are called upon to preach and practice truth. It is our duty to light as well as to love each other, and deal justly by all.

Yet our own nation in her greatness, with her commerce upon every sea, and her name *popular* over the world, with a class of her citizens rich as Crœsus, while others are robbed of their wages, has in effect said: Who is God that we should fear him? Are we not rich? Are we not learned? Are we not .powerful? Do we not build magnificent churches and worship the bones of the prophets? Therefore we care not for man, the child of the Most High.

Have we not said, protect the rights of *property* and sustain the statutes made by us, even if man is crushed?

Jesus taught that institutions, states, nations, churches and Sabbaths were made *for* man—not man for *them*.

Have we not defied that teaching, and made property greater than man?

Let us cite the case of The People *vs.* Toynbee, in the great State of New York, decided by her highest court. (13 *N. Y.* 378.)

In that case a white person owned a black bottle, about twelve inches long and three inches in diameter, filled with intoxicating liquor, worth about two dollars, which was seized by the police, and destroyed by direction of the magistrate in Brooklyn, in pursuance of the statutes of New York. That court declared the statute unconstitutional, on the ground it invaded the right of the individual.

At this same time, and daily, colored men, with the light of divinity in their faces, were dragged through the larger half of our country as slaves. Millions were in this condition. By the power of brute force they were captured and kept from the reach of arms wherewith to defend themselves.

They were denied the privileges of education and their other God-given rights, and kept in ignorance.

By force and fraud they were robbed of their earnings, and treated as beasts of the field.

The idle man rioted upon their productions, in defiance of justice.

The least effort made by the slave prisoner, for his liberty and rights, was defeated by taking his life.

In short, the iniquity of the country in sustaining such an institution, was too monstrous to be described or realized.

Yet how few of us saw the condition of the poor slave, and fed him when he was an hungered, or clothed him when he was naked, or visited him in his prison bonds, or even spoke a kind word in his behalf in the pulpit or in the forum.

While the highest court of the great civilized State of New York in effect held the possession of the black bottle to be a sacred right, the highest court of this christian nation, enrobed at Washington, decided that the black man had *no* rights, and the nation could not hear his cry for justice and liberty.

"Matter was made for man, and not man for matter."

Yet we had thus in our insolence exalted property above man, and set God and his laws at defiance.

The student must have read history in vain, not to see that the same general principles which were applicable to ancient nations, are equally applicable to ours.

Those wise utterances of the ancient prophets, who were true statesmen, are equally applicable to this day and nation.

Let us consult their teachings, and trace the result upon those people who refused to heed them.

Of Babylon, the Almighty, through Isaiah, spake:

"I will punish the world for their evil, and the wicked for their iniquity ; and I will cause the arrogancy of the proud to cease, and will lay low the haughtiness of the terrible.

"I will make *man* more precious than fine gold.

"And Babylon, the glory of kingdoms, * * shall be as when God overthrew Sodom and Gomorrah.

"It shall never be inhabited, neither shall it be dwelt in from generation to generation." (13 *Isaiah.*)

But our worldly conservatives say: We are wiser than of old. We have our great city of New York, with a million of inhabitants, and with ingenuity to make ships and weapons to conquer the world. Why should we fear God, and be compelled to do right?

So said the men of Babylon, only two thousand four hundred and three years ago. She far exceeded New York in population, wealth and power, and was built upon a river fifteen hundred miles in length, while our Hudson is less than three hundred.

But where is Babylon now?

Exactly where New York will be within two hundred years from this day, unless we repent as a nation, and cease fighting against God, and let his children be free.

We need go no further back than Jamestown, to verify this prophecy. Two hundred years since it was a prosperous town upon the banks of the James river, teeming with commerce and slavery.

Now, there is not a building left, to show where it reared its proud head.

"The greatest fall of man is sinning against the light of God placed within his own spirit.

" To sin against is to knowingly violate.

" If a man know of a truth that which his Father requireth, yet of himself goeth directly opposite thereunto, great is the fall of that man."

All slave-holders do not necessarily fall under this condemnation. By education many have been led to believe that it was right to enslave persons of color. Many of the noblest men and women of our times have been slave-holders. As individuals they could do scarcely nothing to undo the heavy burthens resting upon millions of their fellows. The huge pyramid of error, ignorance and selfishness upon them was so vast, that nothing but the volcano of war could shake its foundation.

Slavery had so debauched the nation, that freedom of speech at the North was in danger.

The doctrine has recently been announced, that those who *preach* or speak against slavery, are as wicked as those who are guilty of treason.

In other words, that Luther, Wesley and Beecher, for preaching against sin and agitating the world, are as guilty as the murderers, pirates and robbers they denounced. That Jefferson and Franklin, for writing against the evils of slavery, were as wicked as the wrongdoers they described.

A nation which will exalt to office men who are thus perverted, can only be purified by fire.

# CHAPTER III.

## The Constitution no Cloak for Slavery: Recognizing Slavery *de facto* does not Legalize or Guarantee it.

Some, who desire to find a cloak for their wickedness, try to shield themselves under the constitution of the United States, and say that in time of peace the majority have no power to do right and cease fighting against the Creator's laws.

In other words, that the general government, created by that constitution, has no power " to provide for the common defence and general welfare of the United States," or to prohibit slavery, polygamy, treason, or the establishment of an aristocracy, or king, provided they are created by a state or county, without the aid of the national government.

Such a construction is a libel upon that wise instrument, and upon the memory of those sainted men who made it.

There is no clause in it upholding or sustaining slavery. There is no clause in it *authorizing* congress to establish slavery, horse-stealing or piracy, or anything *else* which shall not be deemed for the general welfare, and there is no clause in it which *prevents* congress from establishing justice and securing the blessings of liberty.

Some suggest that slavery is right because Jesus did not specially denounce it by name.

The same argument would sanctify burglary, because he did not specially mention that as against the golden rule.

It is also suggested by some that slavery is protected by the constitution, because it existed when that instrument was framed.

Piracy, murder and other crimes then existed, and were expected to linger with mankind for generations to come, yet such facts then existing is no argument that the constitution meant to protect crime.

But recognizing the existence of slavery *de facto* does not *legalize*, *sanction*, or in any manner guarantee its existence.

In 1772, the famous case of Somerset *vs.* Stewart was decided by Lord Mansfield, in the Court of King's Bench, England. In his decision he held that slavery had no legal existence in England. He said :

"So high an act of dominion must be recognized by the law of the country where it is used. The state of slavery is of such a nature that it is incapable of being introduced on any reason, moral or political, but *only by positive law.* It is so odious that nothing can support it but positive law." (*Howel's State Trials.*)

Previous to this decision, slavery had existed in England *de facto.* The trade in men and women had constituted an important item of commerce. Laws had been passed authorizing their sale on execution ; in fact everything had been done, by all the departments of the British government, to regulate, recognize and sanction human slavery that they could do, short of actually establishing it by *positive law.* In 1697, 8, 9, 10, William III., chap. 26, the parliament of Great Britain had recognized its existence, by encouraging the slave trade as "beneficial" and "advantageous" to the kingdom, and spoke of the importation of negroes into England, where they were held as slaves. The act itself was entitled, "An act to settle the trade to Africa."

Again, in 1749, the parliament of Great Britain passed "An act for extending and improving the trade to Africa," commencing with this preamble :

"Whereas the trade to and from Africa is very advantageous to Great Britain, and is necessary for the supplying the plantations and colonies thereunto belonging with a sufficient number of negroes at reasonable rates, and for that purpose the said trade ought to be open and free to all his majesty's subjects. Therefore be it enacted, &c."

A written constitution or statute is intended to carry out the object of the makers. The framers of our constitution had read the New Testament, were in the habit of praying for the cause of justice, and many of them had signed the delaration of July 4, 1776. They professed to be christians, and were endeavoring to establish a government upon the christian basis, which declares that we should do unto others as we would that others should do unto us.

Therefore *their* constitution must be interpreted with those great principles as our lights.

Many cases can be cited, decided by our most eminent jurists, holding that our constitution and laws are to be construed in the light of christianity.

A judge imbued with this spirit will thus construe that instrument.

It is claimed by those taking an opposite view, that art. 4, sec. 2, sub. 3, gives the right to hold slaves.

That section is treating mainly of the rights of individuals, and placing restrictions upon the states.

Subdivision 1 says: "The citizens of each state shall be entitled to all the privileges and immunities of citizens in the several states."

· The Attorney General has recently decided, what the courts had never denied until recently, that a colored man is a citizen.

Subdivision 3, relied upon, does not use the word slaves. It merely says that no person held to service or labor, escaping into another state, "shall, in consequence of any law or regulation therein, (that is, by any law of such state,) be discharged from such service or labor." It does not say that he shall not be discharged under a law of congress, or that congress shall not prevent states from creating slaves.

If congress prohibits slavery, or if by the martial law slavery has ceased to exist, of course there will be no slaves to escape, and of course none to surrender or deliver up.

"No state shall make anything but gold and silver coin a tender in payment of debts." Yet congress is not thereby prohibited from doing that act.

Since this was written, the Supreme Court of New York have decided this question in the case of Hayne vs. Powers. In that case the court lay down this rule:

"To say, as matter of judicial construction, that a limitation and restriction upon the power of an inferior, by a superior, implies the same limitation and restriction upon the power of the superior, would be in the last degree unwarrantable, without any known rule of construction. The mere statement of such a proposition is its sufficient refutation."

Sub. 2 of the same section declares: "A person charged in any state with crime, who shall flee to another state, shall be delivered up," &c.

It might as well be said that this clause recognizes crime, and therefore authorizes it, as to say the other clause, sec. 3, recognizes slavery, and therefore authorizes it.

Jesus said: "For ye have the poor always with you." As well might be claimed as recognizing poverty, and hence if a poor man was like to earn too much, if colored, he might be robbed of three-fourths of his earnings, for fear he would become rich, and we might have no poor men left to sustain the Bible.

On the contrary, the constitution declares its object to be "to establish justice *and* secure the blessings of liberty."

To accomplish that object, art. 1, sec. 8, sub. 1, expressly declares, congress shall have power "to collect taxes &c. ; to pay the debts and provide for the common defence and *general welfare* of the United States."

Sub. 17 of the same section provides that congress shall also have power " to make all laws which shall be necessary and proper for carrying into execution the foregoing powers, and all *other powers*, vested by this constitution in the government of the United States, or any department thereof."

It is plain, therefore, that if the general welfare requires us to establish peace, and protect the lives of our fellow citizens, and for that purpose to prohibit slavery, congress has full power to do so. Under the same power the government has bought Louisiana and Florida. Under the same implied power it has built forts and cast weapons of war. If all these were deemed necessary for the common defence or general welfare, who shall say that the extermination of slavery is not equally so ?

The government has as much right to use the public money to pay loyal men for slave property emancipated, as it would have to pay for the construction of fortifications, provided slavery is fully exterminated in principle and power, so as to leave the nation safe, and make the common defence complete.

What is for the *general welfare* of mankind, we are aware, has always been, to a certain extent, a disputed question, and probably will continue to be until each man is in the millennial condition.

In regard to all overt acts or conduct, government is instituted to control the actions of individuals, and its decision must necessarily be final, so far as human tribunals are concerned. In the language of Calhoun, " This controlling power, wherever vested, or by whomsoever exercised, is *government*."

Each individual must obey or be punished.

If human statutes or governments require what the individual conscience does not approve, he is not bound to obey, but has the full right to follow the higher law and become a martyr.

True, he may lose his life, but he has saved his soul. He fears not those who kill the body, but rather fears to fight against God and his own conscience.

Therefore, if the government determine that the general welfare requires slavery to die in order to secure the objects of the constitution, one of which is to "insure domestic tranquillity," there is no appeal from such decision except to those who have the right of suffrage.

Laws have been passed at every session since the government was organized, which could only be sustained under that general clause, or as *implied* powers, and which are not within any of the other specified grants of power.

As progress has been made in many things, so the present day of trial in this nation has educated the government to look to its powers and duties. In the language of Judge Marshall, in the McCullouch case, "The question respecting the extent of the powers actually granted is perpetually arising, and will probably continue to arise as long as our system shall exist."

The important acts of the last congress, which have been passed almost unanimously, and are sustained by the great majority of the people, are valid only upon the construction of the constitution herein stated. Does not the same power which gives congress the right to enact what is called the conscription law, also give the right to prevent war and domestic insurrections by abolishing slavery?

When our constitution was framed, its makers were aware that it would not execute itself, that it must be executed by men, and that its construction from *time to time would be according to the condition of intelligence in the masses.*

They were also aware that man or his institutions had not yet arrived at perfection. They conceded slavery was an evil, and soon expected to see a people virtuous enough to do away with it.

That idea is conceded by Jefferson in his letter on slavery to Edward Coles, written August 25th, 1814, wherein he says:

"I had always hoped that the younger generation, receiving their early impressions after the flame of liberty had been kindled in every breast, and had become, as it were, the vital spirit of every American, that the generous temperament of youth, analogous to the motion of their blood, and above the suggestions of avarice, would have sympathized with oppression wherever found, and proved their love of liberty beyond their own share of it. * * * Yet the hour of emancipation is advancing in the march of time. It will come; and whether brought on by the generous energy of our own minds, or by the bloody process of St. Domingo, \* \* \* is a leaf of our history not yet turned over." (*Randall's Life of Jefferson, vol.* 3, *p.* 644.)

All were aware it could not long exist under this government, unless the constitutional rights of the white race were invaded by "*abridging the freedom of speech or of the press.*"

The history of the world proves that great truths uttered by a single individual will revolutionize the opinions of mankind, if they have a fair opportunity for promulgation.

Hence, within the past thirty years, the advocates of slavery have changed their tactics.

Conceding slavery to be a sin, they knew it could not exist under the full light of a free press and free speech. Since that time, therefore, they have taught in their schools, presses and churches, that slavery was right and divine. Whoever would not subscribe to that doctrine was banished or killed.

All contrary doctrines were excluded from the people.

Fortunately for humanity this country produced Calhoun, a man great and bold enough openly to promulgate those doctrines. He seemed to be raised up by Providence for this great work. He was too honest to be a hypocrite, too pure in his intentions to be afraid, too great to be despised. He was the only man, North or South, with sufficient power and influence to unite the advocates of slavery upon a platform broad enough to take issue with justice.

To sustain slavery in his view, he denied it to be a sin. To sustain that proposition he denied that the *colored person* was a *man.*

Conceding such person to be a man, his whole argument falls to the ground, and his construction of the constitution gave congress full power to abolish slavery.

If this great man could not demonstrate that the general government had not power over slavery, it would seem folly for us to doubt it.

The human race have not yet reached the end of knowledge, and have reasonable grounds to expect further progress in that direction. When Fulton discovered the wonderful powers of steam, and promulgated the same to the world, succeeding generations did not remain idle, but have profited by his experience, and added their improvements to the great stock of wisdom for the benefit of mankind.

Jesus preached his doctrines more than 1,800 years since, and yet for the first 1,500 years, and up to the time of Luther, no man was permitted to enjoy freedom in religious matters.

If the princes, potentates, and rulers of this world, in church and state, so falsely or ignorantly construed christianity for 1,500 years, is it remarkable that the princes of slavery and selfishness in this nation should have falsely construed the constitution for 70 years past.

# CHAPTER IV.

## The Union represents the only Sovereign Power.

There can be but one supreme power. There can be but one sovereignty and but one nation within the same territory.

That sovereignty in this nation is represented by the general government.

" This constitution and the laws of the United States, which shall be made in pursuance thereof, shall be the SUPREME LAW of the land; and the judges in every state shall be bound thereby, anything in the constitution or laws of any state to the contrary notwithstanding." (*Art.* 6, *sec.* 2.)

That government must construe its own powers.

If an individual or state alleges that the legislative branch of such government has overstepped its powers, some tribunal must decide that question.

That tribunal is the Supreme Court of the United States, established by the general government.

State sovereignty is an impossibility under the above-clause. Hamilton distinctly so stated in the convention, and his view substantially prevailed. (*Secret Debates, page* 129.)

The existence of state *powers* or state *rights*, and individual rights, is fully conceded, but it is a misnomer to call a state a *sovereign power*. The people made both governments, and they made the one supreme and sovereign, and the other inferior and subordinate. The same distinction exists as between the supreme court and an inferior court in all judicial systems.

It is true the people did not give full or absolute power in all matters to the general government, neither did they give such power to the state government.

Where the people had not restrained themselves by the national constitution, they were at liberty to give the residue of the governmental power to the state. In no case have the people given all of such residue to any state government. Certain inalienable rights of the individual are not granted to any government in this country.

There is no doubt that many and vastly important rights are left to the state, and by many eminent men state sovereignty has been assented to, but upon examination it will be found to be as impossible as two kings with supreme power over the same kingdom, or two generals commanding the same army, each with supreme power.

The very proposition shows its own absurdity. The devil might as well be compared with the Almighty, and both declared to be supreme. We might as well confound truth with falsehood, right with wrong.

In mathematics it might as well be asserted that a circle has two centres.

Previous to July 4, 1776, these colonies made no claim to sovereign power or to existence as a nation, or separate nations. The sovereign power was then vested in Great Britain. When we separated from her it was by the joint act of all the people within the colonies.

We assumed the position of an independent nation, not as several nations. As a unit we fought, succeeded, made peace, and were recognized among the family of nations.

Hamilton, in substance, concedes this doctrine. After quoting the closing part of the declaration, he says:

"Hence we see that the union and independence of these states are blended and incorporated in one and the same act, which, taken together, clearly imports that the United States have, in their origin, full power to do all acts and things which independent states may of right do, or in other words, full power of sovereignty." (2 *Hamilton's works*, 358.)

In the old articles of confederation, the experiment of a nation with several heads was tried.

In the second article it was declared: "*Each state retains its sovereignty, freedom, and independence.*"

Experience soon taught that we were not one nation, and had no government by which to prevent war and violence between the several states.

The present constitution was adopted within a few years after, by which we were united as one nation, and in which no such words were retained; but it professes to be made by "the people of the United States," and to be made for "the United States of America" as a nation, not for "the several states in their sovereign capacity."

In the language of Ch. Justice Marshall, delivering the unanimous opinion of the Supreme Court in the case of McCullouch *vs.* The State of Maryland:

"The government of the Union, then, is emphatically and truly a government of the people. In form and in substance it emanates from them. Its powers granted by them, and are to be exercised directly on them and for their benefit." (4 *Wheat.*, 316; 4 *Condensed R.*, 466.)

The people being made one nation, a government to protect and maintain it became a necessity, therefore a matter of divine ordination.

A disquisition on government by Calhoun, is probably the ablest work ever written on that subject. He there says:

"There is no difficulty in forming government." "Necessity will force it on all communities in some form or another."

"Constitution is the contrivance of man, while government is of divine ordination. Man is left to perfect what the wisdom of the Infinite ordained, as necessary to preserve the race."

"Governments must be able to repel assaults from abroad as well as to repress violence and disorders within." (*The works of Calhoun, vol.* 1, *p.* 8.)

"Exigencies will occur in which the entire powers and resources of the community will be needed to defend its *existence*. When this is at stake, every other consideration must yield to it. Self-preservation is the supreme law as well with communities as individuals." (*Ib., page* 10.)

Applying these doctrines to the present condition of affairs, can we doubt that not only the general welfare of the United States, but its self-preservation as a nation, gives the government full power to remove all institutions or obstacles in the way of that object?

Paley says:

"There necessarily exists in every government a power from which the constitution has provided no appeal; absolute, omnipotent, uncontrollable, arbitrary and despotic."

To show that the people of that generation had no doubt of the power of congress to prohibit slavery, or do anything else for their general welfare, we refer to the amendments to the constitution proposed at the first session of congress in 1789, and soon after ratified by the states.

"Of these amendments, article 1 provides:

"Congress shall make no law respecting an establishment of religion or prohibiting the free exercise thereof, or abridging the freedom of speech or of the press, or the right of the people peaceably to assemble and to petition the government for a redress of grievances."

This amendment was voted for in congress by the great men who had framed the constitution, and it was approved by Washington. By adopting it they conceded that without it congress had implied power to do the acts therein prohibited. It was foreseen that congress being the judge of what was for the general welfare, might abolish slavery, establish a church, or abridge the freedom of speech.

Where matters are thus left to the legislative discretion, it is well settled that the courts cannot review that discretion and declare such acts void.

In the language of the court in the case of McCullouch *vs.* The State of Maryland, above quoted :

"But where the law is not prohibited, and is really calculated to effect any of the objects entrusted to the government, to undertake here to inquire into the degree of its necessity, would be to pass the line which circumscribes the judicial department, and to tread on legislative ground. This court disclaims all pretensions to such power." (4 *Cond. R.*, 482.)

Hence the necessity of this amendment taking away from congress the power and discretion of making certain laws, but not taking away the power to prohibit slavery and leaving congress the full judge of its own powers, *where not restricted.*

To show that the matter was not overlooked, but was intended, by referring to the discussions in the convention called by Virginia to ratify the constitution, it will be found that Gov. Randolph then said :

"I hope there is none here who, considering the subject in the calm light of philosophy, will make an objection dishonorable to Virginia ; that at the moment they are securing the rights of *their citizens* an objection is started, that there is a spark of hope that those unfortunate men now held in bondage may, by the operation of the *general government*, be made free."

The above construction is in effect given by the supreme court in the case last cited.

"That this idea was entertained by the framers of the American constitution, is not only to be inferred from the nature of the instrument, but from the language. Why else were some of the limitations, found in the ninth section of the first article, introduced ? It is also, in some degree, warranted by their having omitted to use any restrictive term which might prevent its receiving a fair and just interpretation. In considering this question, then, we must never forget that this is a *constitution* we are expounding." (4 *Cond. R.*, 473.)

Thomas Jefferson, in his Notes on Virginia, speaking of slavery, says :

" And can the liberties of a nation be thought secure when we have removed their only firm basis, a conviction in the minds of the people that these liberties are the gift of God ? That they are not to be violated but with his wrath. Indeed, I tremble for my country when I reflect that God is just, and that his justice cannot sleep forever.

"But we must wait with patience the workings of an over-ruling Providence, and hope that that is preparing the deliverance of these our suffering brethren. When the measure of their tears shall be full—when tears shall have involved heaven itself in darkness, doubtless a God of justice will awaken to their distress, and, by diffusing a light and liberality among their oppressors, or at length by his exterminating thunder, manifest his attention to things of this world, and that they are not left to the guidance of blind fatality."

The present war is that exterminating thunder in the hands of man, guided by Providence.

Did George Washington, while he was helping to frame this constitution, understand that he was throwing the sanctions of the national government around an institution which he declared ought to be abolished, and that his vote should not be wanting for that object ? Hear him in his letter to La Fayette :

" The benevolence of your heart, my dear Marquis, is so conspicuous on all occasions, that I never wonder at fresh proofs of it. But your late purchase of an estate in the colony of Cayenne, with a view of emancipation, is a generous and noble proof of your humanity. Would to God a like spirit might diffuse itself generally into the minds of the people of this country."

Again, to Robert Morris :

" There is not a man living who wishes more sincerely than I do to see some plan adopted for the abolition of slavery. But there is only one proper and effectual mode by which it can be accomplished, and that is by legislative authority ; and this, so far as my suffrage will go, shall not be wanting."

Did Dr. Franklin think the constitution he had just assisted in drafting had, by its guarantees, bound the federal government to sanction and sustain that institution which he was then so earnestly praying them to destroy, and which prayer, in 1790, was repeated in these words ? " that congress would take measures 'to secure the blessings of liberty' to the people of the United States, without distinction of color."

Did he understand that the national government had no power conferred upon them to grant the prayer of his petition, and was he praying in mockery of their weakness?

Did Mr. Madison think he was building an eternal wall of defence around that institution, by the guarantees of the constitution, when he said "it would be wrong to admit the idea that there could be property in man." Was he a man that would impose upon the national government an obligation to sanction, sustain and defend an institution like the one he described in the very first congress, under the constitution, May 13th, 1789:

"I should venture to say it is as much for the interest of Georgia and South Carolina (to abolish the slave trade) as of any state in the Union. Every addition they receive to their number of slaves tends to weaken them and render them less capable of self defence. In case of hostilities with foreign nations, they will be the means of inviting attack, instead of repelling invasion. It is a necessary duty of the general government to protect every part of the empire against danger, as well external as internal. Everything, therefore, which tends to increase this danger, though it may be a *local* affair, yet, if it involves *national expense or safety*, it becomes a concern of *every part* of the Union, and is a proper subject for the consideration of those charged with the general administration of the goverment."

Did Judge Wilson think the constitution of the United States had, by its sanctions and guarantees, become the bulwark of slavery, when he told the people of Pennsylvania "that it had laid the foundation for banishing it out of the country?"

Mr. Calhoun, in the last speech he ever made, (March 4th, 1850,) in effect conceded this power of congress to abolish slavery, and also conceded that unless something was done to convince the country that *slavery was not a sin*, that it would be abolished by the general government throughout the states.

On the next day Mr. Foote, of Mississippi, dissented from Mr. Calhoun, and contended that the South could hold their slaves in defiance of the general government, without any amendment of the constitution; and Mr. Calhoun reiterated his assertion, that without further guarantees, "that unless there be a provision in the constitution to protect us against the consequences, the two sections of this Union will never live in harmony."

The last administration approved a resolution, March 2, 1861, which had been passed by both houses of congress, saying no future amendment should be made to the constitution authorizing congress to abolish slavery.

This resolution was conceived in fraud, and intended indirectly to smuggle into the constitution a restriction upon the power of congress, where none had before existed.

There was no other excuse for such an amendment. If congress was already restrained in that matter, such proposed amendment was wholly unnecessary; and the amendment could be annulled in the future by the same power that made it.

Fortunately the people have not yet ratified that amendment.

Our unworthy agents were willing to put the yoke upon thirty millions of people, which should attempt forever to hold the poor in bondage; but before the people had time to perfect that iniquity, God sent this war upon them for their good, and just in time to save them.

By proposing that amendment, congress indirectly admitted the existence of such power, otherwise the amendment was unnecessary.

John J. Crittenden and nearly all the great lights of slavery gave that construction by voting for such amendment.

It is said that a committee of congress, at its first session, denied such power, on the petition of Dr. Franklin and others, that congress should step to the very verge of its constitutional power in opposition to slavery.

Suppose they did, were the committee wiser than Franklin, Washington and Madison, who made that constitution? That committee and other politicians ever since have sought the votes of slave-holders, and hence have caused their opinions to conform to the opinions of those who would continue them in office.

When the occasion demands it, the eyes of the people will be so far opened as to see that power clearly given.

Daniel Webster, in his celebrated reply to Mr. Hayne, January 26, 1830, said:

"This government, from its origin to the peace of 1815, had been too much engrossed with various other important concerns to be able to turn its thoughts inward."

It may truly be said that since that time this nation has been so intent upon raising cotton, building railroads, and increasing its material prosperity, that it has not found time to be just until war had called us to reflect.

All earthly laws and institutions are made by human beings, and the higher their development, the more just will be the laws they will promulgate.

# CHAPTER V.

## SLAVERY IS WAR.

WE have seen that the day comes to all nations, institutions and individuals, when they are to be tried in the light of Truth and Right. When we were in a state of partial peace and of material prosperity, we refused to listen to God and our consciences. Ever since we announced to the world, July 4, 1776, the rights of man, we have failed practically to assert them. A state of war has existed here ever since. A war of the rich against the poor black. What is war? As defined by all authors, it may be a contest between nations by force, or any other state of contest between large parties by violence.

If a single individual seizes another, and takes his goods by force, society calls it robbery. If he takes his life, we call it murder.

If a large number associate together, and by force take from others, society calls it war. Therefore slavery is war. Large numbers of persons have associated, and by force taken the liberty and labor of the poor and weak. That state of war has continued over seventy years, but the African race, and those having a sprinkling of their blood, have until recently been the only victims.

But as sure as God reigns, the whole' human family are bound together by one invisible tie, centring in the Creator, and no wrong can be inflicted upon the least of these without affecting all, sooner or later.

> " Is true freedom but to break
> Fetters for our own dear sake;
> And with leathern hearts forget
> That we owe mankind a debt?
> No! True freedom is to share
> All the chains our brothers bear,
> And with heart and hand to be
> Earnest to make others free."

We may flee into the wilderness, and the same principle is there. We may surround ourselves by high walls, and shut our eyes and ears, but our conscience is here. We may go upon the mountain-top—lo! God is there.

As a necessary result, this institution of slavery has now raised its demon head, and extended its war against the white race as well as the black.

Mr. Boyce, of South Carolina, said in 1851 :

" I object, in strong terms as I can do, to the secession of South Carolina. Such is the intensity of my conviction upon the subject, that if secession should take place, I shall consider the institution of slavery doomed, and that the great God, in our blindness, has made us the instruments of its destruction."

England did not secure the rights of her people by " Magna Charta," A. D. 1214, until, in the language of his historian, " the tyrant John had ravaged the country in a most dreadful manner. The inhabitants were tortured, massacred and pillaged, and their castles, towns and villages burnt."

Nothing else would awaken the conservative and the down-trodden to assert their God-given rights.

Slavery has already—

1. Debauched most of the public men of the nation for forty years past.

2. It has kept four millions of the white race at the South, in ignorance, wickedness and poverty.

3. It has made tyrants of the great majority of its leaders.

4. It has corrupted public opinion throughout the North, to an extent to hinder the progress of civilization.

5. It has made us a stumbling block in the eyes of the liberals of all Europe.

6. It has made us weak and less respected in the eyes of foreign governments.

7. It has deprived over three millions of our fellow beings of freedom, in defiance of God and his laws, and in direct violation of the constitution made by us for their protection as well as ours. Even this was not enough to arouse the nation; and slavery has,

8. Added a thousand millions to our debt, and millions to our taxes.

9. It has butchered in cold blood thousands of white persons residing within its locality, for not raising the hand of treason.

10. It has butchered in battle over one hundred thousand of our sons and brothers who have gone forth to fight for our freedom, and left widows and orphans scattered over the land, with sorrows too sacred to be spoken ; and it defiantly intends to butcher more, unless we take its life.

Thus our nation is being tried by fire and blood, because nothing else had or would produce a state of humility and justice in our minds.

Yet nothing else would give us courage to attack that profane and wicked prince of slavery, whose day is come, and when iniquity shall have an end.

"Thus saith the Lord God : Remove the diadem, and take off the crown; exalt him that is low, and abase him that is high." "I will overturn, overturn, overturn it; and it shall be no more, until he come whose right it is, and I will give it to him."

Thus this nation is about to remove the diadem from slavery, and agitation will continue until that result is attained, and our laws shall be made upon the principles of our constitution and of right, and our judges shall decide in accordance with justice. When Presidents and other officers act upon that principle, then he has come who has a right to rule, and we can truly be called a christian nation.

# CHAPTER VI.

## The Proclamation the great Event of the last Eighteen Hundred Years.

Looking at the history of the world in this light, the Proclamation of January 1, 1863, is the greatest event within the last eighteen hundred years.

If our people are sufficiently educated by war, suffering and mourning, it will be sustained, and for the first time on earth we shall realize a government founded upon eternal principles of right, where the low are exalted, and all are secured in the rights which they have inherited from their Creator. Upon no other foundation can nations expect success.

When slavery fired its first gun upon the white race on this continent, April 11, 1861, this people were not prepared to do justice and ask God to take their side. On the contrary they said, we care not for him, or for his oppressed children. We have countless hosts, brave men, and will put down the war upon us, and leave it in full fury against the down-trodden race.

When the Union army was about to cross the Potomac in May, 1861, Gen. Mansfield, its commander, issued an order that no slave should be permitted within its lines. That order raised a direct issue with the Almighty, forgetting that "He is present wherever his child is found."

Like Sennacherib of old—

> "The Assyrian came down like a wolf on the fold,
> And his cohorts were gleaming in purple and gold;
> And the sheen of their spears was like stars on the sea,
> When the blue wave rolls nightly on deep Gallilee.
>
> "Like the leaves of the forest when summer is green,
> That host with their banners at sunset were seen;
> Like the leaves of the forest when autumn hath blown,
> That host on the morrow lay withered and strown."

The true prophet expected the disaster at Manassas, as soon as that order was issued. That same commander afterwards was slaughtered by slavery upon the field of battle.

3

Thus the nation has struggled on for nearly two years, trying to conquer without God on their side.

What should we have gained by crushing, even exterminating, every man enrolled in its army, as long as slavery, in spirit and power, remained to poison our institutions?

The same as man would gain, if he heaped up silver like dust, and yet lost his own soul.

While the country in great part was mourning over the last disaster at Fredericksburgh, in December, the angels above saw it was a *necessity*, and that without it, the proclamation of January 1st would never have been born.

It seemed like a last dreadful struggle to succeed without asking the aid of the God of Battles, by doing justice to the oppressed.

Instead of desponding, the country now has reason to rejoice and be exceedingly thankful for many things.

We have a President far above any that the nation deserved. He has obeyed the still small voice within his conscience, and dared to do right, although surrounded by the wicked of this world. He cannot himself now appreciate the blessings which posterity will shower upon him for his sublime proclamation.

The same spirit that has sustained slavery in this nation, has hatched forth every other vice known to man. Among others, it has foisted into place and power, the hypocrite and the selfish man— the man who worships the golden calf, and the slimy politician.

The seat of government, where so much money and patronage are dispensed, necessarily attracts the most corrupt of that class.

" Where the body is, there will the eagles be gathered together."

That this nation has been so fortunate as to see an honest man— one who loves truth and right—elevated to the head of this government, seems providential.

The representative is ordinarily no higher in character and principles than the majority of the body by whom he is selected. Hence but few honest men obtain office.

They cannot consistently resort to those corruptions generally necessary to secure place.

Occasionally some sudden turn of events or unforeseen emergency will put forward a person intelligent and just beyond his peers or his constituency.

Such a man was placed at the head of this nation, for this great trial.

Like all men chosen by Providence for great occasions, in his youth he mingled with the poor, and received his education mainly from that inspiration which an honest intent is sure to bring.

Yet we must remember that any man standing alone is weak, and may not be able to resist, at all times and forever, the evil influences surrounding him.

It therefore becomes every lover of good order and right to sustain him by proclaiming these truths to the country.

We cannot have peace until we are willing to be just and truthful.

Before high heaven we declared, in 1776, " that all men are created equal."

Upon our knees before the Almighty, with that profession we called for his aid, and were answered.

After long success we forgot our vows, and through Chief Justice Taney denied that we intended what was then said.

In the Dred Scott decision he said:

"The general words above quoted would seem to embrace the whole human family, and if they were used in a similar instrument at this day, would be so understood. But it is too clear for dispute, that the enslaved African race were not intended to be included."

Thus adding falsehood and hypocrisy to our crimes, while robbing the poor of their liberty.

This was said in direct conflict with a previous decision of the same court in Gibbons *vs.* Ogden (9 *Wheaton*, 1, 209), where it is laid down as the rule on this point, that the framers of the constitution " must be understood to have employed words in their natural sense, and to have intended what they said ; * * * that there is no other rule, than to consider the language of the instrument * * * in connection with the purpose for which it was used."

As we have seen, the day now has come when we are commanded to repent.

We are also commanded by God to " speak *every* man the truth to his neighbor." (8 *Zach.*, 16.)

That command is addressed to all. Can we honestly be silent?

We appeal to the clergy—that class who mould the education of the world—to speak forth in trumpet-tones in favor of God and human rights. " Cry aloud and spare not, and show my people their transgressions."

We appeal to the lawyers—that class whose profession leads them to advocate the right and defend the helpless—to speak forth on this great occasion in behalf of those who are not allowed to speak for themselves.

> " They are slaves who fear to speak
> For the fallen and the weak."

The ladies have a great mission to perform. While the men fight the battles of their country, the ladies have a higher and holier mission to perform—that of educating the country to love justice and do mercy to all classes and races, until they realize that—

"God hath made of one blood all nations of men to dwell on all the face of the earth." (17 *Acts*, 26.)

# CHAPTER VII.

## The Nation, through Congress, must settle this Question.

Upon congress, as the law-making power of the nation, the greatest responsibilities rest.

Mighty questions will arise in the history of a people which are too great to be settled by the courts.

In the contest between Henry and Edward, for the crown of England, to suspend the civil war, Henry, then in possession of the crown, proposed to leave the question of the right and title thereto to the judges of the King's Bench. Edward readily consented, knowing he would run no risk. If the court decided in his favor he was satisfied that Henry would acquiesce. If they decided against him, Edward intended to take the crown by force, without regard to the decision of the judges.

Upon that case the judges returned the celebrated answer: "That they had no jurisdiction of the question; that the nation only could decide who was the true King."

Alexander Hamilton seemed to have been designed by Providence with sufficient foresight to shape this government broad enough to meet all emergencies.

As early as September 3, 1780, in a letter to James Duane, he used these prophetic words, while we were living under the articles of confederation, with no central power to make one nation:

"The defects of our present system, and the changes necessary to save us from ruin. * * * The fundamental defect is a want of power in congress." (*Hamilton's Works, vol. 1, p.* 150.)

Seven years afterwards, experience and necessity gave birth to our present constitution, which united us into one nation, and gave those additional powers to congress.

That constitution was adopted for all time, with no right of secession.

When certain delegates in the convention of New York were talking about a conditional ratification to settle that question, in July, 1788, Madison wrote to Hamilton:

" A conditional ratification is not valid. * * * The constitution requires an adoption in *toto* and *forever*."

With that construction put upon it in advance by one of its chief creators, it was ratified, and secession is not countenanced.

By frequent elections all necessity for revolution by force is avoided.

Through a convention, the majority of the electors can modify the constitution without bloodshed or commotion.

Notwithstanding it was foreseen that great emergencies might arise which would call out the full powers of government to preserve us.

The supreme court have said:

" This could not be done by confiding the choice of *means* to such narrow limits as not to leave it in the power of congress to adopt any which might be appropriate, and which were conducive to the end. This provision is made in a constitution intended to endure for ages to come, and consequently to be adapted to the various *crises* of human affairs." (4 *Cond. R.*, 478.)

That crisis is upon this nation now. All the nations in the world recognize it.

Our supreme court have recently decided in the case of the Schooner Brilliant, &c. *vs.* The United States, that the blockade is valid, and among the implied powers which the President may exercise on such occasions. The court say:

" They cannot ask a court to affect a technical ignorance of the existence of a war, which all the world acknowledges to be the greatest civil war known in the history of the human race, and thus cripple the arm of the government and paralyze its powers by subtle definitions and ingenious sophisms." (*Am. Law Reg.*, vol. 2, *p.* 339.)

The last congress passed many acts which will live in history as among the wisest devised by man. Yet more remains to be done.

When the cohorts of Satan desire to defeat justice or sustain vice, every one of their votes are given boldly for their cause.

Would that those in congress, who profess to love freedom and equal rights, had equal courage and would act up to their convictions of duty and leave the consequences to God.

The rebel states, by their own act, have voluntarily repealed, so far as within their power, their birth and existence as states.

Congress could repeal the several acts admitting such states, and remand the same to the condition of territories.

Although they would thereby lose their condition as states in the Union, yet the land would remain under the jurisdiction of congress, upon which new territories could be organized.

If any inhabitants remain therein who do not like a republican government, construed practically in favor of justice and freedom, there is no clause in the constitution forbidding their migrating to a more congenial country and associations.

The magnitude of the questions now involved, shows that they can only be settled by the majority of this nation. The army alone cannot do it. The South alone cannot do it. The nation alone has the power.

We have tried compromises with Satan and slavery, but peace did not come.

In the language of Calhoun, in his last speech in the senate, but a few weeks before his death:

" Having now shown what cannot save the Union, I return to the question : How can the Union be saved ? There is but one way by which it can with any certainty, and that is by a full and final settlement, on the principles of JUSTICE, of all the questions at issue between the two sections."

" Such a settlement would go to the root of the evil and remove all cause of discontent." (*Works of Calhoun, vol. 4, p.* 571.)

" At all events, the responsibility of saving the Union rests on the North and not on the South. The South cannot save it by any act of hers, and the North may save it without any sacrifice whatever, unless to do justice, and to perform her duties under the constitution, should be regarded by her as a sacrifice." (*Id.*, 572.)

We are aware that in Mr. Calhoun's argument he assumes a colored person is not a man, and therefore has no claim to justice. Correcting that *fact*, and conceding the African race to belong to the human family, and Mr. Calhoun shows us the only true solution of this crisis.

The responsibility is upon the North. The South is weak, and they intentionally gave the general government the power, and it only remains for the North " to perform her duties under the constitution," by declaring freedom to all men, and thus carry into effect the object of the constitution, " by establishing justice, securing the blessings of liberty, and insuring domestic tranquillity."

# CHAPTER VIII.

## A State cannot Legally make a Slave.

It is suggested by some who desire the right, that although the proclamation has put an end to slavery in South Carolina, and no slave is now held legally within her borders, yet that South Carolina as a state, after the Union is restored, can establish slavery, and make slaves of free men.

If a state has such power, of course it is not restricted to *color*, and it can make slaves of such portions of the white race as the majority, by physical force, shall determine.

Any government, which is not restricted by a written constitution, and is sustained by a majority of its people, has the physical *power* to enact any law, no matter how unjust.

The true object of government, as ordained by the Creator, is simply to protect the individual against wrongs.

Whenever each person becomes just, he will be a law unto himself, and do no wrong to his neighbor. Then there will be no occasion to resort to government for protection.

The form of government may nominally remain, but it will become obsolete, and the execution of active powers will be no longer evoked.

Until then, the Mosaic law is a necessity, and the strong arm of government will be required to enable society to exist and perfect itself.

As long as governments are administered by imperfect beings, so long will they be liable to abuse.

To prevent that abuse, the most proper and reliable safeguard is the right of suffrage, and the right to change rulers at reasonable times by election, thus avoiding the necessity of a revolution. (*Works of Calhoun, vol.* 1, *p.* 12–14.)

As the majority would thereby have the power to oppress the minority, or weaker races, unless restrained, a written constitution, with guarantees and restrictions, becomes a necessity for the protection of the latter.

It is a fundamental principle of our government that natural rights, such as life, liberty, &c., are inalienable and supreme, and above the authority of all governments; that governments are institutions of the people for the *protection* of these rights and liberties, and that it is incompetent for them to enact laws for their destruction. Hence the presumption always is, in cases of doubtful interpretation, that the legislature intended to do or require nothing contrary to natural right and justice; and unless the language of the enactment is so clear and explicit that it is impossible to avoid the contrary conclusion, the courts are bound so to interpret them; or, to use the language of the Supreme Court of the United States, in the case of United States *vs.* Fisher (2 *Cranch*, 390): "Where rights are infringed; where fundamental principles are overthrown; where the general system of the law is departed from, the legislative intent must be expressed with irresistible clearness, to induce a court of justice to suppose a design to effect such objects."

The proposition maintained by law writers is this:

"No government or authority whatever can do that which is subversive of the ends for which it owes its existence."

Puffendorf says, "that it is God who imposed the law of nature upon the human race, and dictated the establishment of civil societies to serve as instruments of enforcing these laws."

Domat declares, "that sovereignties can have no other rights but such as have in them nothing contrary to the use which God requires them to make of said power. The sovereign power can only be legitimately exercised for the *end* to be obtained, and that end is the protection and preservation of the lives, liberties and property of the citizens, and not for the destruction of either. That the wise and the good and the just is the circle of the divine law, within which the human sovereignty must move; that the law being the embodiment of all perfection and justice, its spirit as well as its letter denies the right of man to do an unjust act, or to infringe upon natural right." (*Domat Pub. Law, B.* 1.)

"The sovereign power can only be called into exercise for the attainment of the great end which that compact was designed to secure, and cannot be converted into an engine to defeat the end mankind had in view. When they entered into their social compact, and the moment this inviolate and sacred rule is departed from, there is criminal abuse of power from which no obligation to obedience can arise." (*Vattel, B.* 4, *secs.* 45, 46.)

John Locke: "Though the legislature be the supreme power, it cannot be arbitrary over the lives and fortunes of the people.

" The legislative power, in the utmost bounds of it, is limited to the public good of society.

" It is a power that has no other *end* than the *preservation*, and therefore can never have a right to *destroy*, *enslave* or designedly impoverish the subject.". (*Locke's Works, v.*.5, *ch.* 11, *p.* 416.) Robert Hall takes the same view, and denies the correctness of the reasoning of Burke and others, who ascribe despotic power to parliament.

The doctrine of the omnipotent power of parliament now only exists in theory. It was denied in effect by William Pitt and Lord Thurlow, in their opposition to the bill annulling the East India Company, in 1783.

In the Supreme Court of the United States, Mr. Justice Chase could not submit to the omnipotence of state legislation, or that it was absolute or without control, although its authority should not be expressly restrained by the constitution. He held " that the people of the United States enacted their government to establish justice, to promote the general welfare, to secure the blessings of liberty, and to protect their persons and property from violation. The purposes for which men enter into society determines the nature of the social compact. As they are the foundation of legislative power, they will determine the proper objects of it." (*Calder* vs. *Bull*, 3 *Dallas Rep.*, 386.)

In Gorham *vs.* Stonington, (4 *Conn. Rep.*,) Hosmer, J., held: "If there should exist a case of direct infraction of vested rights, too palpable to be questioned and too unjust to be vindicated, he could not avoid considering it a violation of the social compact, and within the control of the judiciary."

In Wilkinson *vs.* Leland, in the U. S. Court, (2 *Peters' Rep.*, 654,) same doctrine held by Webster and sustained by the court.

In the Supreme Court of South Carolina, (1 *Bay's Rep.*, 252— *Bowman* vs. *Middleton*,) it set aside an act of the legislature as being against common right, on the ground that it took away the freehold of one man and vested it in another, without any compensation or any previous attempt to determine the right, declaring the act *ipso facto void*.

Again, the same court held that a statute framed against common right and common reason, was so far void as it was calculated to operate against those principles. But they said the court would not do the legislature that injustice, to say that such was their intention.

and therefore would give it such a construction as would be consistent with the dictates of natural reason, though such construction might be contrary to the letter of such statute.

It being the well settled theory of our government, as before observed, that men's *na'ural rights* are the true basis of all governmental power and authority, and the *inalienability* of those rights the *limits* of that authority, hence when the American judge is called to sit in judgment upon an enactment of the legislature, it is his first business to see that the subject of enactment is within the scope of the constitutional authority of the legislature. He will then construe the act, if possible, to mean nothing inconsistent with the natural and inalienable rights of man. But if he finds the language too clear and explicit to admit of any other construction, he will next examine into the constitutional authority by which such a particular law was enacted; and if the constitution does not in direct, positive and unequivocal terms thus authorize such legislation, the judge will hold the law to be unconstitutional and void. But if, on examination, he should find an express, unequivocal grant of authority in any state constitution to pass laws destructive of liberty and the rights of man, he would then hold the grant void, for want of authority in the people to make such a grant; for to admit the right of the people to establish a government destructive of the rights of man, is to deny the *inalienability* of those rights, which is to deny the authority of the people to establish a government in defence of them, and thus deny the source of all governmental authority, except what proceeds from brute force.

" What in principle constitutes a despotism ? It is where the will of an individual or individuals is placed above the rights of man, and arms itself with power to crush the individual; and it matters not in principle whether that will originate in a single individual or in twenty millions. The will and the power to crush the individual constitutes the despotism."

Fortunately, our constitution of the United States forbids any state government to execute despotic powers.

In addition to the well settled principles of liberty, before quoted from common law authority, the constitution of the United States expressly prohibits the making of a slave. Article 5 of the amendments expressly declares that "no person shall be deprived of life, liberty or property, without due process of law."

Due process of law, ever since the days of Magna Charta, has been defined to mean a trial and conviction, in the courts in the ordinary course of the law, for a wrong done or crime committed.

The legislative authority, under that constitution, does not even extend to taking a foot of land from one person and selling it to another.

The New York Supreme Court, in Taylor vs. Porter, by Judge Bronson, held:

" That though no constitutional inhibition interfered, the legislative power did not reach to such an unwarrantable extent. That neither life, liberty or property, except when forfeited by crime, or when the latter is taken for public use, falls within the scope of its power, and that when it steps beyond the bounds of its power, its acts, like those of the most humble magistrate in the land, are utterly void." (4 *Hill.*)

While slavery existed *de facto*, it might be argued that the slave was not deprived of liberty, because he never had any to lose.

If that argument is sound so far as the border states are concerned, it can have no application in those states where the proclamation has already made them legally free.

If in defiance of the constitution, of right, and of the laws of God, the legislature of South Carolina can make a single person a slave, then, indeed, there is nothing to restrict it from following the precedent of Herod, and enacting that all male children, under a certain age, shall be slain. Before this war is closed, God will so educate this people that they will, for their own protection, see that the constitution shall not again be violated by making a single slave within our borders.

# CHAPTER IX.

## THE NATIONAL GOVERNMENT BOUND TO PROTECT EVERY PERSON WITHIN ITS BOUNDARIES.

BUT conceding that such state has no just power or constitutional authority to make a slave, it is asked how the nation can prevent it? By the same power that the nation proposes to collect the duties at Charleston and disperse the rebel armies at Richmond. The general government is bound to execute every right guaranteed by the constitution.

The Supreme Court of the United States have in several instances recognized this doctrine.

In the case of Prigg *vs.* The Commonwealth of Pennsylvania, the court have said :

"If the constitution guarantees a right, the natural inference certainly is, that the national government is clothed with appropriate authority and function to enforce it." Again : "The fundamental principle applicable to all cases of this sort, would seem to be that where the end is required the means are given ; and where a duty is enjoined the ability to perform it is contemplate to exist on the part of the functionaries to whom it is entrusted." (16 *Peters*, 615.)

Again :

"The national government, in the absence of all positive provisions to the contrary, is bound, through its own proper departments, legislative, judicial and executive, as the case may require, to carry into effect all the rights and duties imposed upon it by the constitution." (*Ib.*, 616.)

And again :

"A right implies a remedy, and where else would the remedy be deposited than where it is deposited by the constitution." And finally : "The end being given, it has been deemed a just and necessary implication that the means to accomplish that end are also given ; or in other words, that the power flows as a necessary consequence to accomplish the end." (*Ib.*, 616.)

"The *executive power* shall be vested in the President." (*Art.* 2, *sec.* 1, *sub.* 1.)

He is enjoined " to take care that the laws be faithfully executed." (*Art.* 2, *sec.* 3.)

That "*power*" is vested in the executive department.

It is impossible to execute that power unless congress by law gives him the means to enforce it.

The *means* placed by congress in the hands of the executive, for the last two years, have been money and *white* men.

So far those means have failed to accomplish the end.

Congress, therefore, have the power expressly given to furnish any and all means necessary, and "to make all laws which shall be necessary and proper for carrying into execution all other powers vested by this constitution in the government of the United States, or in any *department* or *officer* thereof." (*Art.* 1, *sec.* 8, *sub.* 17.)

The enactments necessary to enable the President to enforce the laws, and preserve the Union, are those which will free every slave, and enroll all able bodied friends, without regard to color, in the armies of the nation.

The principles laid down by Ch. J. Marshall, as the unanimous opinion of the Supreme Court, in the case of McCulloch *vs.* The State of Maryland, fully sustain this doctrine. (4 *Cond. R.*, 473.)

In that case the court say :

"There is no phrase in the constitution which, like the articles of confederation, excludes incidental or implied powers ; and which requires that everything granted shall be expressly and minutely described.

"A constitution, to contain an accurate detail of all the subdivisions of which its great powers will admit, and of all the *means* by which they may be carried into execution, would partake of the prolixity of a legal code, and could scarcely be embraced by the human mind."

Hamilton, as Secretary of the Treasury, in an official letter to President Washington, February 23, 1791, takes the same view :

"That every power vested in a government is in its nature sovereign, and includes, by force of the *term*, a right to·employ all the *means* requisite and fairly applicable to the attainment of the ends of such power, and which are not precluded by restrictions and exceptions specified in the constitution, or not immoral, or not contrary to the essential ends of political society." (*Vol.* 4, *p.* 105.)

Calhoun concedes the same doctrine :

"None can deny that the government of the United States has the power to acquire territories, either by war or treaty; but if the *power* to acquire exists, it belongs to congress to carry it into execution." (*Works of Calhoun, vol.* 4, *p.* 564.)

Yet no one will pretend that there is any express clause authorizing congress to acquire territory. It is an inherent power of sovereignty. Jefferson doubted it. He thought the general government had no more authority to acquire Louisiana than it had to abolish slavery.

The proclamation having been issued as a war measure by virtue of the " *power* " vested in the executive as commander-in-chief, we have seen that congress has full authority to pass all laws to carry that power into effect.

The Supreme Court say upon that subject, at page 478 of the case last cited :

" The subject is the execution of those great powers on which the welfare of a nation essentially depends."

Upon the expediency and necessity of that proclamation, the executive is the only judge. (4 *Cond. R., p.* 477.)

To enact laws to make it effectual, devolves upon congress.

Proper for that purpose would be a law allowing every slave the benefit of the writ of habeas corpus, and all other measures to insure his future freedom.

Such laws could be executed as soon as we are ready to collect the direct taxes in the rebellious territories. To aid in that work, the slaves will be more necessary, than was the United States Bank, to transmit the taxes after their collection.

The constitution guarantees rights to each individual, as follows :

1. "The privilege of the writ of habeas corpus shall not be suspended," unless in rebellion, &c. Yet slavery has suspended it for the last fifty years.

2. "The citizens of each state shall be entitled to all the privileges and immunities of citizens in the several states."

Yet no citizen of a Northern state could in the South read the declaration of independence or the Bible to the bondmen, or be allowed the freedom of speech in the presence of white men.

3. "The United States shall protect each state against domestic violence."

Slavery says no. It will have domestic violence at the expense of the old and the young.

4. "The rights of the people to be secure in their persons, houses, papers and effects, against unreasonable searches and seizures, shall not be violated."

Slavery says it will seize without right or warrant.

5. "No person shall be deprived of life, liberty or property without due process of law."

For seventy years past slavery has said, we defy your constitution and will hang white men without either process or law.

6. "In all criminal prosecutions the accused shall enjoy the right to a speedy and public trial, by an impartial jury."

Slavery says the white man shall have neither, but shall be hung without trial or jury.

It is therefore evident the white person can never be secure in his constitutional rights as long as slavery lives.

Those who desire to excuse vice say, why not leave the slavery question to Providence instead of the government?

Why not leave forgery, slavery, robbery and other crimes to Providence?

If society, through the law and by means of government, has no right to protect the weaker race against slavery, it has no right to protect the weaker man against the highwayman.

It has been suggested that the proclamation only frees the slave during the war, and that after the restoration of peace he may be legally captured by authority of the state and returned to bondage.

As well might ships captured, condemned and sold be reclaimed after the war. Who supposes that our officers and soldiers will be held liable in a state court, after the war is terminated, in trespass for property taken for the army or bridges burned? Title acquired or divested by acts of war is as conclusive as by judicial sales. This is not an open question.

The slave once emancipated legally remains so forever. Nothing but brute force can re-enslave him, and no nation worthy of existence will ever tolerate it.

Nothing could more surely degrade us and sooner produce our downfall, unless we shall basely ask the negro to fight for our Union and then leave him unprotected in the hands of his tyrant master, without shielding him by the constitution and laws.

Every person compelled to obey a government is entitled to its protection.

# CHAPTER X.

## A Republican Government, as guaranteed by the Constitution.

We find in the 4th section of the 4th article of the Constitution of the United States the following guarantee:

"The United States shall guarantee to every state in this Union a republican form of government, and shall protect each of them against invasion; and on application of the legislature, or of the executive when the legislature cannot be convened, against domestic violence."

Here we find a guarantee of a republican form of government to every state in the Union.

This clause has generally been understood to guarantee to every state in the Union, as such state, that each of their sister states should sustain a republican form of government; and that it was the right of each state, under the federal constitution, to demand that the government of every other state in the Union should be republican in form. But this is not the real meaning of that clause, although the effect of it will be to secure to each state a republican form of government. It has a meaning more vital to the cause of human freedom, and one that bears more directly upon the sacred immunities of the American citizen than such a construction could possibly give to it.

We must again recur to the question, who made the constitution of the United States? The answer is, the people. Who made the several guarantees therein contained? The people. With whom were they made? With one another; each with all and all with each; they are the mutual guarantees of all and each. For what purposes were they made? "To establish justice, insure domestic tranquillity, provide for the common defence, and secure the blessings of liberty to themselves and their posterity."

All these guarantees are joint and several in their character. Let it, then, be constantly kept in mind that the people of the United States, in their original sovereign capacity as individuals, were the only parties to this instrument. That as such, they, in the exercise

9

of their native sovereignty, formed this constitution, and made with each other-the guarantees therein contained for their *mutual* and *individual* protection.

The great Hamilton takes the same view when he says:

" The constitution is a compact made between the society at large and each individual. The society, therefore, cannot, without breach of faith, and injustice, refuse to any individual a single advantage which he derived under that compact, no more than one man can refuse to perform his agreement with another." (*Hamilton's Works, vol. 2, p. 322.*)

The States, as such, were no parties to that instrument, although through the people they were all parties to it. To the states, as such, no guarantees were made, although, through the people composing the states, all the guarantees were made to them. Let these things be kept in mind in fixing the meaning and force of this guarantee of a republican form of government to every state.

With this view, we say this guarantee was designed to be a pledge of all the people of the Union to each individual ; that the relation which the state government should ever bear to him should be that of a republic ; that is, that its treatment of him as a subject of that government should be consistent with the principle that it was *his* government, as established by *his* authority, for the protection of his natural, inherent rights. We say it was a guarantee to the *individual*, not to the state as such, not to the *voting people* as such, nor to a majority of them, but to ALL, whether enjoying the franchise of suffrage or not.

We repeat, it is not a guarantee to all the states in the Union that each particular state government shall be republican in structure ; but it is a guarantee to all the people of each state that their particular state government shall be of a republican character.

Is it asserted that the intention of this guarantee is only to secure each state in the Union against the inconvenience and danger of allowing any other than republican governments to be united with them ? We answer, if that were their only intention they signally failed to express it. The language used expresses no such intention. Had they only said, the United States shall guarantee *that* every state in this Union shall be of a republican form of government, such an intention might have been claimed with some degree of propriety ; but when they said, " The United States shall guarantee to every state in this Union," &c., it means quite another thing.

By the language used, the guarantee of a republican form of government is either *to the state*, as such, or to the people composing the state; and it is that *their* particular form of government shall be republican.

But it was not to the state, as such, that the guarantee was made. Because in the first place: The states, as such, stood in no need of such guarantee. The people of the state had full power at any time to determine the particular form of their own government, whether oppressive or just, liberal or despotic ; and if they desired a republican form of government, they could have whichever they chose, without any guarantee whatever from the national government. It cannot be said that the majority of the people wished to be secured against *their own future volitions*, which might, on failure of their present system, demand a different form of government; and yet the doctrine that the guarantee was made to the state, as such, would imply that. No, it was not the *state*, but the *individual*, crushed and overwhelmed by an insolent and tyrannical majority, that needed such a guarantee ; and to him, as a citizen of the United States, whether in the majority or minority, is that guarantee given, to secure him not only from *individual* but also from *governmental* oppression.

And, in the second place: This guarantee was not made to the state, as such; because if it were so, should a majority of the state resolve to change the form and structure of their government, in other words, to annihilate it and establish another, that being or subject to whom the guarantee was made would cease to exist, and there would be no one left to receive the enforcement of it, unless by *scire facias* the new government should be made a party to the guarantee.

And in the third place: The states, as such, were not parties in the formation of the national government, and therefore would not be subjects of guarantees from the people of the United States, except through the people composing the state.

All the ends sought to be accomplished by the formation of the national government are better secured by considering this guarantee as made with all the people of the several states, securing to each the benefit of a republican form of government, and pledging to them the faith and power of the nation that their relation to the state government shall ever be that of free citizens, for whose benefit and by whose authority, in common with their fellow citizens, that government was established and to be administered. By giving this construction to that clause, we not only secure to each individual the benefits of a republican form of government, but we secure the same to each state, and also to all the states, that every state in the Union shall possess a government republican in form.

And this construction is sustained by a decision of the Supreme Court of the United States; they say:

" If by one mode of interpretation the right must become shadowy and unsubstantial, and without any remedial power adequate to the end; and by another mode it will attain its just end and secure its manifest purpose, it would seem, upon principles of reasoning absolutely irresistible, that the latter ought to prevail."

The only objection that can be urged to this construction is, that it gives to all the citizens of the United States the benefits of a free government, and brings them all within its absolute protection.

Hamilton says:

" The rights, too, of a republican government are to be modified and regulated by the principles of such a government. These principles dictate that no man shall lose his rights without a hearing and conviction before the proper tribunal ; that previous to his disfranchisement, he shall have the full benefit of the laws to make his defence." (*Hamilton's Works, vol. 2, p.* 320.)

He also uses this language in the Federalist, No. 52:

" The definition of the right of suffrage is very justly regarded as a fundamental article of republican government."

We are aware that the section of the constitution under consideration has never been executed by a general law of congress, applicable to all of the states. It has frequently been applied to new states when they are admitted, and as a fundamental law such states have been forever prohibited from establishing or tolerating slavery.

The executive department acted under it in the case of the Dorr rebellion in Rhode Island. Upon that question Chief Justice Taney used this language:

" It rested with congress, too, to determine the means proper to be adopted to fulfill this guarantee." (*Luther* vs. *Borden,* 7 *How.,* 42.)

The Supreme Court have settled the same doctrine in the celebrated case of Prigg *vs.* The Commonwealth of Pennsylvania, before quoted. In that case it is expressly held that:

" If the constitution guarantees a right, the natural inference certainly is, that the national government is clothed with appropriate authority and protection to enforce it." (16 *Peters,* 615.)

That decision was made under the clause of the constitution in regard to fugitives from service, but in which no express declared powers were given to the general government on that subject.

True, many of the friends of freedom put a different construction upon that clause, but they were overruled by the great body of American statesmen and lawyers—by the majority of the people, and by the unanimous opinion of the Supreme Court.

The minority were compelled to submit or become martyrs.

The nation are therefore now estopped from denying the same powers to the general government, under a clause of the constitution substantially the same. The same rule should be applied in both cases, even if the great emergency now upon us shall verify the prediction of Randolph and secure entire freedom in America through the agency of the general government.

In execution of section 4, article 4, congress has power, by law, to define and declare:

1. What is a republican form of government as applied to each state. It should not be left to the executive as heretofore, in the case of Rhode Island, to decide, but should be previously regulated and settled by law, so that all could understand their duties.

2. How a state should be organized, giving the loyal people the right to legally and formally elect their executive and two branches of the legislature, even if their existing officers should abdicate, as they have recently done by secession. This power was only intended to be exercised by congress in the last resort.

If such power does not exist in the general government, then a majority of the state *legislatures,* against the wishes of three-fourths of the people, can at any time break up the general government. No such construction can be tolerated by any government.

This view is partially recognized by Hamilton in the Federalist, No. 59, where he says:

" Its propriety rests upon the evidence of this plain proposition, *that every government ought to contain in itself the means of its own preservation.*"

The last congress, to a certain extent, carried out this principle in the case of West Virginia.

3. That the electors, to choose the most numerous branch of the

state legislature, shall at least include the great majority of male inhabitants of the proper age.

This principle is also recognized in No. 57 of the Federalist, as follows:

"The elective mode of obtaining rulers is the characteristic policy of republican government."

"The electors are to be the great body of the people of the United States."

We are aware that many of the framers of the constitution, and even Hamilton himself, did not claim the power of congress to extend to defining the qualification of electors; but wisely they used language which would cover such power.

No man can foresee all the great consequences which in the future may turn upon acts which at the time seem unimportant to him. Hence it frequently happens that their acts, writings or laws are wiser than they intend.

Our constitution seems to have been framed by an unseen wisdom, and experience has shown and is now demonstrating that it is not "a covenant with hell," but the charter of true liberty.

This doctrine is also clearly recognized by the Supreme Court of the United States in the case of Martin vs. Hunter's Lessees, reported 1 *Wheat.*, 304, and also in 3 *Cond. R.*, 550.

In that case the court say:

"It was foreseen that that would be a perilous and difficult, if not an impracticable task. The instrument was not intended merely to provide for the exigencies of a few years, but was to endure through a long lapse of ages, the events of which were locked up in the inscrutable purposes of Providence. It could not be foreseen what new changes and modifications of power might be made indispensable to effectuate the general objects of the charter; and restrictions and specifications, which at present might seem salutary, might in the end prove the overthrow of the system itself. Hence its powers are expressed in general terms, leaving the legislature, from time to time, to adopt its own means to effectuate legitimate objects, and to mould and remodel the exercise of its own powers as its own wisdom and the public interests should require."

4. That no state law should be enacted to take away from any person (of any color) his right to life, liberty and property, without due process of law; and that each person shall be entitled to the benefit of the writ of habeas corpus to protect him in his liberty.

5. That no state law should be deemed republican or valid creating slavery.

Any law or state regulation in opposition to such national laws would be void, and any individual injured could submit his case to the highest court in the United States to have conflicting laws construed.

.We are aware that this power given to the general government has never been exercised by congress, but that is no reason why it should not be when the occasion arises.

Slavery and polygamy are fast forcing upon the nation questions which will compel it to assert its undoubted powers in that behalf.

·We are in the midst of the greatest war known in the history of the world. The field of battle is located within this favored nation.

It must necessarily work a great moral revolution. Providence has given us the occasion. Shall we not grow strong and perfect what it has placed in our hands ?

If we survive this struggle and perfect our freedom by ridding ourselves of slavery, we shall become the great nation of the earth, and our example will guide all others.

War will be known no more among us. A future war between this country and any nation of Europe would be improbable.

Our whole powers could then be turned towards developing a higher civilization and perfecting man for an eternal existence.

Is not such a result worth our effort ?

We have the aid of the prayers of three millions of the oppressed.

Shall not our prayers mingle with theirs and ascend to heaven, asking for this great blessing ?

# CHAPTER XI.

Rules of Construction. The Declaration of Independence Estops the Nation from Continuing Slavery.

Much is said about early history and cotemporaneous opinions, to
aid in construing the constitution.

Mankind are entitled to the experience of the past, and cannot
wisely shut their eyes to its teachings. But all wisdom has not departed with any man or generation. If so, the continuation of the
human race might properly be suspended.

It has been said : " Be ye therefore perfect, even as your Father
which is in heaven is perfect."

The eye of faith can see in the distance the time foretold, when
"they shall not build, and another inhabit; they shall not plant,
and another eat."

It would seem, therefore, to be true wisdom to consult all the
results of the past, and try to improve for the future.

With this view, the opinions of Madison, Hamilton, Franklin, and
those other great men who put forth our constitution, should have
great weight in arriving at its meaning. We are aware some of the
great men of those days did not claim that congress had full power
over slavery.

But it must be remembered that they were merely the *opinions of
individuals*, and do not *estop* the nation from giving a broader or
deeper construction, as the exigencies of the case shall require.

Not so with great fundamental *acts* by which a nation is brought
into existence. The declaration of independence was such an act.
It spoke in behalf of the people. They based their authority upon
the equal common rights of man. They claimed all their powers by
virtue of their common humanity, and by that claim accorded to all
other men the same rights and powers.

By denying to the government of Great Britain the rightful power
to violate these privileges in their own persons, they denied to *themselves* the rightful power to violate them in the persons of others ;
and by this solemn act of theirs, they are forever estopped from set-
ting up such claim.

The declaration of independence was a solemn deed of acquittance of all rightful power to violate the natural and inalienable

rights of man, acknowledged before God, in the presence of the world. That deed of acquittance contained the following covenants:

1st. That "life, liberty and the pursuit of happiness" are gifts from God to man, and therefore the natural and inalienable right of all.

2d. That governments "derive all their *just* powers from the consent of the governed," and are established for the protection of these natural rights.

3d. That when governments become destructive of these ends, for which they are established, they act without authority, and the people are at liberty to resist them and throw them off.

4th. That when the government evinces a design to disregard the ends of justice, and reduce her subjects under absolute despotism, *it is their duty* to overthrow such government and establish new guards for their future security.

Who were they that thus executed this great deed of acquittance? For and in whose behalf was it thus executed?

They were the representatives of the thirteen *united* colonies, in general congress assembled, and they assumed to do it in the name and by the authority of the good people of these colonies.

They were inspired by all that was noble, great and true; and as those venerable men sat in that hall, and one by one executed that deed for freedom, the sacred stillness of that hour betokened the audience of angels.

Then they rose above the mortal, and *uttered forth the law of God.*

The day on which it was published became an era in the world's history. There was no battle fought or victory won by force of arms; but it was a day made holy by the advent of the great doctrines of *universal freedom.*

Thus we have seen that the inalienable right of all men to liberty was proclaimed by the representatives of the thirteen united colonies, in congress assembled, in the name and by the authority of the good people of those colonies; that the people ratified the proclamation in the most earnest and solemn manner, and that by so doing they have denied to themselves the power to trample upon the rights and liberties of their fellow men.

According to their views, there must be a true source of all political power, and there must necessarily be a *limit* to all political power in all just governments. This source of power was the people; the limit of that power was the inalienability of the rights of man. Hence they repudiated the dogma that governments possessed absolute despotic power, or could possess any such power, for the people had no such power to delegate. Government could never legitimately trample on the rights of man, for the twofold reason, first, because it could never rightfully acquire any such authority; and secondly, such action must be destructive of the ends for which government was created, and would reinvest the people with all their original authority.

Let this, then, be remembered, in construing the constitution formed by these men, who, for themselves and the people they represented, disclaimed all such authority, and we shall find that no language found in that instrument, no force of circumstances, no historical proof—not even all combined—can make that instrument legally sanction or guarantee human slavery.

Taking these rules, then, for our guide, and we have only to find the *guarantees* of the constitution to insure the protection of every citizen in the enjoyment of his natural and inherent rights. For *in* those guarantees we find plenary power to enforce them.

If the constitution of the United States was formed for the purposes of establishing justice among its citizens; to provide for the common defence of its citizens; to promote their general welfare; to secure to them the blessings of liberty; and these guarantees were made for that end, then most unquestionably the federal government has full power to secure these ends through the proper departments thereof. If laws are to be made to enforce these guarantees, we have a national legislature to enact them: if adjudication is to be had, we have a national judiciary: if they only remain to be executed, we have a national executive clothed with the power of the whole Union. What, then, is or can be necessary to secure to all the full benefit of these guarantees?

The only thing wanting for the protection of every individual in the full enjoyment of his natural and constitutional rights, is a disposition on the part of the people to enforce the guarantees of the constitution. Let them no longer plead that they *would* do it if they *could.*

They have the full power, and if they neglect to repent and do justice, the great laws of the Ruler of the Universe will sooner or later bring them into that condition, although it be through mourning in every household, after a baptism of blood.

# CHAPTER XII.

## THE PRESENT AGE CALLS TO A HIGHER DUTY.

UNDER the last administration the government had so low an appreciation of its powers or duties, that it dare not defend its own arsenal, but in Charleston turned it over to the state for safe-keeping.

After the inauguration of President Lincoln, for some time all was doubt and uncertainty.

The diplomatist and conservative were disposed to lie down and tamely submit to disunion and slavery.

"All experience hath shown that mankind are more disposed to suffer, while evils are sufferable, than to right themselves by abolishing the forms to which they are accustomed."

In the same spirit the government hesitated, and the slumbering patriotism in the masses had not been called forth, and it was expected that Fort Sumter would be evacuated.

In this hour of doubt and hesitation, a private citizen, through Senator King, addressed the government, March 23, 1861, in which were the following suggestions:

"1st. It seems to me, the evacuation of Fort Sumter will be a practical recognition of the Southern confederacy.  *  *  *

"2d. It gives up the whole ground, and compels the United States to take the affirmative—declare war in effect—to regain a foothold within the seven Southern states, whereas by standing fast, it compels the traitors to strike the first blow against the regular army, and will thus turn the whole loyal sentiment of the country against them.

"3d. If the President does all in his power to reinforce Major Anderson with the navy at hand, his duty is fulfilled, and the country will sustain him. If he tamely evacuates, the whole loyal sentiment is weakened, and the Republican party will be overwhelmed at the North.

"4th. What human nature admires and demands, is courage and truth, and whenever the man at the helm shows the right spirit, he will be sustained and strengthened.  *  *  *

"Let this commotion go on—the curse will fall upon Sodom."

The attempt to reinforce Fort Sumter followed. The first gun of slavery produced upon the country the desired effect.

Yet the government seemed to hesitate about using its powers to coerce the rebellious slave power.

It seemed to doubt its right to order the army across the Potomac upon state territory.

Fortunately, the cession of Alexandria back to Virginia, brought the state line near the capital.

When it became apparent that the long guns of the rebels, from Arlington Heights, could batter down the capital, the nation became converted, and the army " invaded the sacred soil." The Rubicon was passed.

Thus *necessity*, that great parent of invention, called into exercise the conceded but dormant powers of the executive.

The constitution says : " The privilege of the writ of habeas corpus shall not be suspended unless, when in cases of rebellion or invasion, the public safety may require it."

Yet in defiance of that guarantee, the writ has been suspended for over seventy years in about half of the United Stetes, so far as colored persons are concerned, and practically suspended so far as white men should assume to plead their cause.

The same *necessity* will yet require congress to pass a law giving to every person the benefit of that writ, without regard to color.

Such right can then be executed through the national courts wherever any state or tyrant shall, without due process of law, assume to hold in bondage any person not convicted of crime.

No resolution of congress, or platform of any party, of a negative character, can become authority upon matters of construction.

Until congress acts *affirmatively*, and enacts the proper laws to perfect freedom, the direct question cannot be decided by the judiciary.

When those acts are passed, and any state or individual shall question them, then, and not till then, is the Supreme Court made the arbiter between the two.

In the language of Webster, in his reply to Hayne :

" Having constituted a government and declared its powers, the people have further said, that since somebody must decide on the extent of these powers, the government shall *itself* decide, subject, always, like other popular governments, to its responsibility to the people."

If, therefore, the Supreme Court shall not decide what honest men think to be right; shall not carry out the object of *the constitution as it is*, " to secure the blessings of liberty," we have no remedy until that court shall be converted, or its members changed, when it will decide according to the spirit of the age.

The horrors of war and the manifestations of divine wrath are fast working such conversion.

When that conversion takes place, and the constitution *"as it was"* shall be truly interpreted *"as it is,"* in the spirit of justice and christianity, instead of being, as heretofore, the fortress of slavery, the Supreme Court will then indeed become the bulwark of FREE-DOM. The habeas corpus, now sighed after by traitors, will then become to the oppressed the angel of deliverance.

All popular governments will necessarily be interpreted to carry out the views of the majority, having the controlling influence. Hence the conversion of the people to a higher sense of justice will call for a more just administration of the government in all of its branches.

To awaken a true sense of freedom and justice in the minds of the masses, seems to require great sacrifices and atonements. Such we have had, and many more are in store for us, until we heed them.

Within a few months past, the rebel authorities seized upwards of twenty colored persons upon a steamboat in Tennessee, who were innocent of all crime—who were not engaged in the war—and, without trial, cause or provocation, took them into the field, in the presence of the civilized world and before high heaven, openly, in the day time, butchered them in cold blood as a sacrifice to the demon of slavery.

When an act of this kind is committed upon a single individual, it is usually done clandestinely, and the perpetrator is so abhorred that he is taken from among men as unfit to live.

Yet the perpetrators of this act are open, and assume to do the crime in the name of the intelligence and organized leaders of slavery.

Such an act has not its equal among the savages.

Such an act in Asia or Africa would startle the world.

Even a single sacrifice of a human being, to conform to a bigoted religion, makes humanity shudder ; while here, we have twenty sacrificed upon the shrine of slavery, and the country has hardly heard, much less condemned it.

The blood of those innocent martyrs has mingled with the waters of the rivers and of the ocean, and is crying to be avenged. Shall we shut our ears and close our hearts longer against their wailings ?

When Governor Wise, the Pontius Pilate of Virginia, hung John

Brown, instead of thereby extinguishing the flames of freedom, it only made them blaze the brighter.

So, adding these children of color to the list of unnamed martyrs, will not retard the downfall of the prince of evil.

Of what avail is our fighting? Of what avail is our teaching? Of what avail is our preaching and fasting, until we have become *doers* of the word? The Almighty, by his prophet Isaiah, has said to us:

" Is not this the fast that I have chosen to loose the bands of wickedness, to undo the heavy burdens, and to let the oppressed go free, and that ye break every yoke?"

"Then shall thy light break forth as the morning, and thine health shall spring forth speedily, and thy righteousness shall go before thee; the glory of the Lord shall be thy rearward."

With such principles as our guide, and the power of God to protect our armies, they will indeed be invincible.

Abraham Lincoln, called under God by the American people to the highest worldly position, has officially obeyed that command.

Shall we hesitate and let all be lost? or shall we act and receive the reward?

If we now fall short of securing entire freedom on this continent, a reaction will take place here, as it did upon the restoration of Charles II. in England, when the friends of humanity were hunted from that nation. Then we should see our brave and true men driven from this country to find an asylum—where?

The hope of the down-trodden of Europe and the rest of the world would be put back for centuries. But humanity will not fail. As sure as God reigns, right will finally triumph.

> ." Earth is waking, day is breaking,
> Darkness from the hills has flown;
> Pale with terror, trembling error
> Flies forever from her throne.
> Then to labor, friend and neighbor,
> With thy soul's resistless might;
> Never fear thee, God is near thee,
> He doth ever bless *the right*."

Lightning Source UK Ltd.
Milton Keynes UK
12 December 2009

147406UK00001B/83/A